WONDER OF THE WORLD

BY
DAVID
LINDSAY-ABAIRE

★

★

DRAMATISTS
PLAY SERVICE
INC.

2

WONDER OF THE WORLD was first produced by the Woolly Mammoth Theatre Company (Howard Shalwitz, Artistic Director; Kevin Moore, Managing Director) in Washington, D.C., opening on May 22, 2000. It was directed by Tom Prewitt; the set design was by Lewis Folden; the lighting design was by Lisa L. Ogonowski; the sound design was by Hana Sellers; the costume design was by Justine Scherer; the fight direction was by John Gurski; the dramaturg was Mary Resing; and the production stage manager was Annica Graham. The cast was as follows:

CASS	Deb Gottesman
KIP	Michael Russotto
LOIS	Nancy Robinette
KARLA	Kerri Rambow
GLEN	Bruce Nelson
CAPTAIN MIKE	Kirk Jackson
BARBARA, PILOT, 3 WAITRESSES and JANIE	Emily Townley

A revised version of WONDER OF THE WORLD was produced by the Manhattan Theatre Club (Lynne Meadow, Artistic Director; Barry Grove, Executive Producer) in New York City, opening on October 11, 2001. It was directed by Christopher Ashley; the set design was by David Gallo; the lighting design was by Ken Billington; the original music and sound design were by Mark Bennett; the costume design was by David C. Woolard; the fight direction was by Rick Sordelet; the dramaturg was Christian Parker; and the production stage manager was Kate Broderick. The cast was as follows:

CASS	Sarah Jessica Parker
KIP	Alan Tudyk
LOIS	Kristine Nielsen
KARLA	Marylouise Burke
GLEN	Bill Raymond
CAPTAIN MIKE	Kevin Chamberlin
BARBARA, PILOT, 3 WAITRESSES and JANIE	Amy Sedaris

CHARACTERS

CASS HARRIS: a woman in her 30s, anxious to start a new life

KIP HARRIS: her husband, also in his 30s

LOIS COLEMAN: a little older than Cass, an alcoholic with a barrel

KARLA: a woman in her 60s, a dabbler

GLEN: her husband, in his 60s, a dabbler

CAPTAIN MIKE: 30s, captain of the *Maid of the Mist*

BARBARA, HELICOPTER PILOT, WAITRESSES and JANIE: all played by one actress

SET

The set, with its multiple locations, should be simple and somewhat representational. Most importantly, nothing should stop the flow of the play.

WONDER OF THE WORLD

ACT ONE

Scene 1

Lights up on Cass packing a suitcase in her bedroom. Nearby a television plays a Marilyn Monroe movie. Cass half-watches the TV while she packs. A door slams offstage. Cass looks up, frozen.

KIP. *(Off.)* Hey sweetie! Guess who's home for lunch?! *(Caught, Cass futilely tries to hide the suitcase. Marilyn Monroe continues to sing. Off.)* Cass? Where are ya? You'll never guess what I got! *(She grabs the remote control and shuts off the TV, as Kip enters the bedroom, carrying a huge gelatinous aspic on a tray.)* Hey, there you are.
CASS. Hi, honey.
KIP. I brought lunch.
CASS. Oh yeah?
KIP. You know what it is?
CASS. *(Looks at it.)* Jello?
KIP. It's aspic. Molded in the shape of a fish.
CASS. Oh. Nice.
KIP. Like in the old movies? Remember you said you wanted to try aspic? It's got chunks of trout in it.
CASS. Since when do you come home for lunch?
KIP. *(Notices suitcase.)* What's that?
CASS. It's a suitcase.

5

KIP. Are we going on a trip?

CASS. Not exactly, no.

KIP. Is this a surprise of some kind?

CASS. I'm leaving you.

KIP. *(Beat.)* Oh. Then it *is* a surprise.

CASS. I'm *so* sorry. I didn't mean for you to —

KIP. You're leaving me?

CASS. You were supposed to be at work.

KIP. You were just gonna run away without telling me?

CASS. I was gonna leave a note.

KIP. Well ... still.

CASS. I'm *really* sorry. I didn't want to have a scene.

KIP. Did I *do* something?

CASS. I don't really want to get into all that. Can you just stand in the corner until I'm done? *(Goes back to packing.)*

KIP. I feel so silly. I brought this aspic.

CASS. I know. This is awkward for me too.

KIP. I combed the city looking for it ... for *you.*

CASS. Oh don't try to butter me up now, Kip. It's a little late for that.

KIP. *(Pause.)* Is this about what I told you last night?

CASS. Can you not mention that please?

KIP. It *is* about last night.

CASS. No, of course not. Really, this has nothing to do with you.

KIP. You don't wanna talk about last night?

CASS. No. My god, you're obsessed with last night. Why'd you have to come home? It makes me want to kick you in the face.

KIP. What?

CASS. I'm kidding. Can you scootch over? I need elbow room to pack. Thanks. *(Cass barely stops moving during the rest of the scene. She's got packing to do.)*

KIP. You understand this is a bit of a shock for me.

CASS. Yes I thought it might be.

KIP. Just last week we walked around the Botanical Gardens and came home and played Yahtzee. I thought we were happy.

CASS. Yeah, that was a lot of fun.

KIP. Then what happened?

CASS. Nothing. I just — *(Apologetically.)* I think I made a mistake.

KIP. When?

CASS. Remember that time you proposed and I said yes?

KIP. Cass —

CASS. I know. It's sad, right?

KIP. That wasn't a mistake.

CASS. Of course *you* think that, but —

KIP. It wasn't.

CASS. But what if it was?

KIP. It wasn't.

CASS. But what *if?*

KIP. It *wasn't.*

CASS. Look, I agreed to marry you based on what I knew to be true. Kip equals X. X will make me happy. Everything added up. Seven years later I find out you're not X at all, you're Z. And if you're Z, then I did the math wrong. Z is no good. I would never have said yes to Z.

KIP. Nonetheless, you can't just — People don't just *leave* their lives.

CASS. Sure they do. People pick up and escape to faraway places every day.

KIP. Whaddaya mean, "faraway"?

CASS. This is turning into a scene. This is what I didn't want.

KIP. Well I'm sorry, but this is all very sudden.

CASS. Life can be like that, I've realized. Like that time I *suddenly* discovered you were an odious monster.

KIP. Hey.

CASS. I'm sorry.

KIP. I thought this wasn't about me?

CASS. I was lying when I said that.

KIP. I thought as much.

CASS. This is hard on me too, you know. Maybe not quite *as* hard, but it's still hard.

KIP. Because a part of you wants to stay?

CASS. Yes. The freakish and cowardly part.

KIP. All right, you're upset with me. I understand that. But we're happy. You can't just run off. Who'll do your Tuesday shift at the food co-op? And what about our book group? And movie night? And what about the kids? Think of your kids.

CASS. They're not my kids. They're my students.

KIP. You have a life here.

CASS. But I don't think it's the life I was supposed to have. It's like … Do you remember that time we were driving to Westchester for that flower show in Fairfield and we got really lost?

KIP. Yes.

CASS. And then we finally saw a sign and you were like, "Hey, Fairfield! We found it!" and we got all happy because we knew where we were? And so we took the exit, but it still didn't *feel* right?

KIP. Uh-huh.

CASS. And it turned out we had somehow ended up in Fairfield, *New Jersey* instead?

KIP. Yes.

CASS. It's like that. *(Beat.)* I thought I knew where I was this whole time, but this morning I took a good look around and suddenly realized I was actually in New Jersey.

KIP. But you're *not* in New Jersey. You're in Park Slope.

CASS. Why are you making me sad? I don't want to be sad. I'm a new person today. I'm happy and bubbly. I'm a tall glass of sparkling cider.

KIP. Since when?

CASS. Since this very second. I'm starting a new life and I'm brimming with expectation! There are possibilities where I'm headed!

KIP. Where's that?

CASS. Port Authority. I'm buying a seat on the first available bus. *(Kip stands in front of the door.)* Kip, what are you —

KIP. Can't you just stay for lunch?

CASS. No, I can't have lunch.

KIP. Just give it a try. *(Holds out aspic.)*

CASS. No.

KIP. One bite.

CASS. Kip …

KIP. Try the fucking aspic! *(Silence.)* I'm sorry.

CASS. I have to go.

KIP. Do you need money?

CASS. I'll use the money my mother left me.

KIP. *(Holds out aspic.)* Here, you better take this for the trip. You might get hungry.

CASS. *(Takes aspic.)* Thank you, Kip.

KIP. So ... if you realize you were right, to say yes when I proposed I mean, then ... maybe you'll come back?

CASS. Oh that's such a nice thought, but I don't think that's gonna happen. Bye-bye. *(She closes her suitcase and exits.)*

Scene 2

Lights up on two bus seats. Cass, with her aspic, is seated next to Lois, who is asleep and has something huge on her lap wrapped in blankets.

CASS. The road signs go by so fast, don't they? Four hundred and sixty-three. My old life is 463 road signs behind me. *(Inhales.)* Don't you love the smell of a bus?

LOIS. *(Eyes closed.)* Don't talk to me. I'm pretending to be asleep.

CASS. That's called playing possum. My husband used to do that to avoid sex. *(Spots a sign zipping by.)* Four hundred and sixty four. *(Back to Lois.)* But I can spot a faker. And you're a little faker. Hey, you wanna strike up a conversation?

LOIS. No, leave me alone.

CASS. My name's Cass. And I just left my husband for very mysterious reasons.

LOIS. I don't care. Stop talking to me.

CASS. I've never been to Niagara Falls before. I *almost* went once. A family trip. But then Kip proposed, so I stayed behind to plan our wedding, and my parents went without me. They hit a beaver on the drive up, lost control of the car, and drove into a ditch. My mother was killed and my father's legs were crushed. Okay, your turn to share.

LOIS. Why can't you sit somewhere else?

CASS. You're a challenge, aren't ya? Well you know what? I'm your challenger. *(Beat.)* Remember when the *Challenger* exploded? That was sad.

9

LOIS. That man saved your life, you know. If he hadn't proposed, you would've been in that car wreck.

CASS. You know what? I thought the same thing for a long time, but now I think if he hadn't proposed, I would've gone with my parents, and yelled "Dad, look out for that beaver!" And my mother would still be alive, and we would've gone on to see Niagara Falls, and maybe I would've met another man, the one I was *meant* to be with, instead of that two-faced deviant I married. *(Realizing.)* Oops, I lost track of the road signs. Oh well, that was getting tiresome anyway. Wanna play Punch Buggy?

LOIS. Are you *on* something?

CASS. No, I'm just excited about all the things I'm gonna do. Is this a conversation? Because if it is, I wanna check it off.

LOIS. Check it off?

CASS. I had this list of all the things I wanted to do in life, but for some reason I put it away when I married Kip. P.S.: Big Mistake. *(Pulls out list.)* Here it is. Number forty-eight: "Strike up a conversation with a stranger." I've never done that before. My mother was always like, "Don't talk to strangers, Cass. Don't talk to strangers." So I never did. And you know what? Now I have no friends.

LOIS. Are you gonna eat that aspic?

CASS. No, you want it?

LOIS. You bet. There's nothing like a good aspic. *(Pulls spoon from pocket and digs in.)*

CASS. I'll read some of my list while you eat. *(Reads from list.)* Number one is "Find your soul mate." Ignore the checkmark. That one's a do-over. Number two is "Learn Swedish." Followed by "Wear a large wig," and "Drive cross-country." You know, I haven't driven in seven years. Kip was always afraid I'd bang up his Volvo.

LOIS. *(Eating aspic.)* What's in here? Bass?

CASS. Trout.

LOIS. Damn, it's tasty.

CASS. *(Returns to list.)* Then we've got, "Have a baby. Wear overalls. Go parachuting." I wanted to get married while skydiving. Kip said that was insane, so we had a church service instead. Our wedding song was "Close to You" by The Carpenters.

LOIS. *(Her mouth full.)* She was anorexic.

CASS. Yeah, sad. *(Back to list.)* "Eat venison. Become friends with a clown." Kip's afraid of clowns, so — "Visit a prison and witness an execution by lethal injection." That's more of a long-term goal. "Go on *The Newlywed Game* — "

LOIS. Oh I *love* that show.

CASS. Me too! Only Kip refused to audition. He found the game crass and divisive.

LOIS. That why you left him?

CASS. On some level, yes. Along with a few ... *other* things.

LOIS. What other things?

CASS. I'd rather not say at the moment. I'm afraid it will shock you. But I did add it to my list. Number 267: "Tell someone about Kip's horrifying betrayal."

LOIS. *I* was abandoned.

CASS. Wow. Like the Lindbergh baby.

LOIS. The Lindbergh baby was kidnapped, not abandoned.

CASS. Or so the authorities would have us believe.

LOIS. You're weird.

CASS. Who abandoned you?

LOIS. My husband. I came home to an empty house and a note which said I was a bad person because I drank too much and crashed cars.

CASS. Hey, *I* almost left a note. But my husband came home for lunch.

LOIS. Good thing. A note is a terrible thing to come home to. I know. The bastard. Ah, fuck him. *(Swigs at a flask.)*

CASS. You ever been to The Falls?

LOIS. Just once. A million years ago. We called it a honeymoon.

CASS. Uh-huh. And what's this on your lap?

LOIS. It's my revenge.

CASS. I see. Is it a bomb of some kind?

LOIS. No. A bomb?

CASS. I was guessing.

LOIS. *(Removes blanket from a large barrel.)* Ta-da.

CASS. Look at that. It's a ... big barrel.

LOIS. Heavy too. My legs fell asleep thirty miles ago. I can't move. That's okay. I always wanted to know what it would feel like to be a paraplegic.

CASS. My father's a paraplegic.

LOIS. I'm sorry. Did I offend you?

CASS. No. I was just thinking that I have his phone number if you have any other questions about what it feels like. *(Beat.)* So. A barrel, huh? You gonna hit him with it?

LOIS. *Hit* him with it?

CASS. Again, I'm just guessing here.

LOIS. Niagara Falls? … A *barrel?*

CASS. Ohhhhh … You're gonna go to *Niagara Falls* with a *barrel.*

LOIS. Right.

CASS. To get your revenge.

LOIS. Exactly.

CASS. Are you gonna hide in it, and then jump out and scare him?

LOIS. Are you a moron?

CASS. If I had a nickel for every —

LOIS. I'm going to go over The Falls.

CASS. *(Realizing.)* Ahhhhh … But you'll die.

LOIS. Ay, there's the rub.

CASS. The rub?

LOIS. Imagine it. Poor Lois bobbing up and down at the bottom of The Falls, surrounded by bits and pieces of a smashed pickle barrel.

CASS. It's a pickle barrel?

LOIS. Ted loves pickles. See, that'll add to the power of it all.

CASS. It's funny, isn't it? I'm starting my new life. You're ending yours.

LOIS. That's *funny* to you?

CASS. Well not funny so much as — *(Interrupts herself.)* Hey, do you wanna be my sidekick?!

LOIS. *What? Sideki* — ? You need to learn how to segue!

CASS. *(Shows her list.)* Look, Number Eighty-one: "Get a side-kick." You can be my Gabby Hayes.

LOIS. I'm gonna kill myself.

CASS. Right, but until then.

LOIS. I have things to do, I can't be —

CASS. I'm not taking no for an answer. From here on out, you're my second banana! *(Points out window at front.)* Hey Gabby, there's a sign! Niagara Falls, 346 miles! Yeehaw! *(Blackout.)*

Scene 3

Lights up on a hotel room.

CASS. Oh look, there's only one bed.

LOIS. I don't take up much room.

CASS. Oooo, let's be lesbians for the weekend.

LOIS. I'm gonna put this barrel in the tub, make sure it's water-tight. *(Goes into bathroom with barrel.)*

CASS. *(Refers to her list.)* Okay, we'll skip the "Lesbian Tryst." Maybe I can jump to "Have sex with a bellhop" instead.

LOIS. *(Off.)* Wait until after I go over The Falls. I don't want to walk in on anything.

CASS. Aren't I irrational? *(Goes to bed and bounces on it.)* Bouncy bouncy bouncy. This is another thing my mother wouldn't allow. Bouncing on the bed. I'm disobeying everyone!

LOIS. *(Entering.)* I can get a separate room.

CASS. No, I like sharing. It's like a slumber party. Eeeeeeeeeek! *(Belts Lois with a pillow.)*

LOIS. *(Frozen.)* Don't ever do that again. My mother was suffocated with a pillow.

CASS. Oh, I'm so sorry. Who suffocated her?

LOIS. No one. It fell on her face while she was sleeping. It was a very large and heavy pillow.

CASS. *(Pause.)* I think someone made that story up.

LOIS. What are you getting at?! My father would never lie. He was a gentle and sweet man, so long as I didn't walk in front of the TV! *(Swigs from flask.)*

CASS. What's in that flask anyway?

LOIS. Nothing. It's empty. After all these years of drinking, I've developed a nervous tic. *(Swigs again.)* See what I mean? I have no control over it. That reminds me, I gotta get me some Jim Beam. *(Lois peruses an old guidebook while Cass hangs clothes in the closet.)* Listen, I know you don't know me or anything, but after I kill myself could you do me a favor?

CASS. I guess.

LOIS. *(Gets pen and paper from nightstand.)* I'm gonna give you my brother-in-law's number. I'm sure Ted's staying there. Can you call him and explain what I've done?

CASS. Sure.

LOIS. And tell him that I was real sorry for being a raging alcoholic, and that I wish I could turn back time. And then tell him that I *can't*, and that I killed myself because he abandoned me, which is an irresponsible and rotten thing to do, and I hope he lives with that festering guilt until he dies! And make that last bit really scary. Say it in a damning deep voice.

CASS. Oh, I ... I'm not so good with voices.

LOIS. No? Well, listen to this. *(Yogi Bear impersonation.)* Hey there, Boo-boo. I'm gonna get me some pic-a-nic baskets. *(Normal.)* It's still rough, but I'm working on it. I've got a number of funny voices. It's good to have projects.

CASS. Yes it is. I make mosaic tabletops.

LOIS. Crafty. I do macramé. Take a look at this. *(Lois pulls a macramé purse out of her barrel. The words "I Love Bingo" have been stitched into it.)* I made it myself.

CASS. It's adorable.

LOIS. Thank you.

CASS. You think you could teach me macramé?

LOIS. Sure. It's real easy once you — *(Suddenly realizes.)* No, I can't teach you macramé! I'm here to kill myself! What's the matter with you?

CASS. Sorry, just looking for things to do.

LOIS. I'm making myself a drink.

CASS. *(Consults her check list.)* Oh here's something. "Ask big questions." You wanna philosophize?

LOIS. Hell no. *(Opens mini-bar.)* Whoa-ho! I've found the motherlode!

CASS. Last month I asked Kip what he thought about the afterlife and he looked at me like I had slapped him.

LOIS. Did you?

CASS. No.

LOIS. Aw, that's too bad. I love stories where women slap men.

They make me laugh.

CASS. I wanna philosophize, like in the old days. You know how people used to sit around and just ponder the mysteries of the universe?

LOIS. No. I don't believe anyone ever did that.

CASS. Of course they did. Before there was TV and crack cocaine. People used to talk to each other. Here, I'll start. Do you believe anything is ever really *meant* to happen?

LOIS. I gotta get some ice. *(Leaves room to get ice.)*

CASS. In high school, I was a lifeguard at the municipal pool, and the only person I ever saved from drowning was Kip. That's how we met. I saved his life. I used to think that was fate, but now I think it was just a coincidence. A coincidence that eventually led to the death of my mother. *(Sound of ice maker outside room.)* So now I'm trying to correct the mistake I made all those years ago, which isn't really possible of course because dead people don't come back to life, at least *I* don't believe they do, and yet … *you* show up, ready to die, and I'm thinking, "Is this some kind of second chance thing?" I bet it probably is.

LOIS. *(Having re-entered.)* Your lips are flappin' but I don't hear no English comin' out.

CASS. I think maybe I'm supposed to save your life. I'm here for you, lady. I've got your back. *(Picks up Lois' guidebook.)* You know what I wanna do tomorrow?

LOIS. I hope it doesn't involve talking.

CASS. First we should go to the Cave of the Winds and the Hurricane Deck, and then I wanna ride on the *Maid of the Mist*.

LOIS. The what?

CASS. *(Shows her book.)* It's the boat that rides around the bottom of The Falls.

LOIS. Oh hey, that sounds fun.

CASS. Better than deep-sixin' yourself, right?

LOIS. Not at all. It'll be good to see the water up close, know what I'm in for.

CASS. I wonder what Kip's doing. I bet it's not nearly as fun as a boat ride. You think he's happy I'm gone?

LOIS. Probably.

CASS. I just wonder if he's happy. *(Lights cross-fade from them to …)*

Scene 4

*Kip sits on another part of the stage. It's night and he's
wrapped in a blanket, sitting in a dark room, lit only by the
blue glow of a television. Kip is sobbing as he watches his wedding video. We hear organ music and Cass taking her vows.*

VOICE OF CASS ON WEDDING VIDEO. I Cass, take thee
Kip to be my lawful wedded husband — *(Kip hits rewind on the
remote control. We hear the tape rewind a little, then:)* I Cass, take
thee Kip — *(Kip rewinds again.)* I Cass, take thee Kip … *(Lights
fade on Kip, crying.)*

Scene 5

*Lights up on a wooden walkway at the base of The Falls.
Steps lead up and offstage to what is apparently the
Hurricane Deck. Cass and Lois enter in yellow raincoats.
They yell over the deafening roar of The Falls.*

LOIS. It's taller than I remember! That's good! Less chance of
surviving!
CASS. It's so loud! I didn't know it would be so loud!
LOIS. What?!
CASS. I didn't know it would be so loud!
LOIS. I can't hear you! I have water in my ear!
CASS. Tilt your head and shake it!
LOIS. What?!
CASS. Tilt your head and shake it!
LOIS. Yes! He's my favorite actor! *(Barbara, a tourist, wearing a*

16

large wig and the same yellow rain coat, enters. She speaks in a Texan accent.)

BARBARA. *(Looking up at The Falls.)* Oh my goodness, would you look at that! *(Takes a picture.)*

CASS. It's big, isn't it?!

BARBARA. Yes! I feel like an itty-bitty ant!

CASS. My name is Cass!

BARBARA. Oh hello, Cass! I'm Barbara!

CASS. This is my friend Lois!

BARBARA. Nice to meet you!

LOIS. *(Pointing into the distance.)* There's the boat! It's big! I hope I don't land on it when I go over!

CASS. My friend is gonna kill herself!

BARBARA. *(Happily.)* Awwww, that's sad!

CASS. Look at the captain! His hat is so cute! Maybe I'll sleep with *him!*

BARBARA. *Ooooo!*

CASS. *(To Barbara.)* Is that a wig?!

BARBARA. Yes it is!

CASS. May I buy it from you?!

BARBARA. Whatever for?!

CASS. I've always wanted one! I'll give you one hundred dollars!

BARBARA. All right! *(They exchange the money and wig. Barbara is totally bald. Lois, unaware of the exchange, turns around and is stunned to see the women changed so radically.)* I have female pattern baldness!

LOIS. Oh!

BARBARA. Cass, that wig suits you!

CASS. *(Wearing the huge wig.)* Yes it does! *(To Lois.)* Do you feel alive?! I feel so *alive* right now!

LOIS. I'm looking forward to everlasting peace in the great beyond!

BARBARA. You're funny, Lois! Funny and sad at the same time!

CASS. I miss Kip!

LOIS. What?!

BARBARA. She misses Kip!

CASS. No I don't! I take it back! I was momentarily insane!

BARBARA. *(Happily.)* I think you're both crazy! *(Glen and Karla*

17

enter, also in raincoats. They are in their sixties. Like everyone, they yell.)

KARLA. Does this walkway lead to the Hurricane Deck?!

CASS, LOIS and BARBARA. Yes!

KARLA and GLEN. Thank you!

CASS. It's beautiful, isn't it?!

KARLA. Breathtaking!

GLEN. We're on our honeymoon!

BARBARA. That's sweet! Elderly honeymooners!

KARLA. We prefer the term Late Bloomers!

BARBARA. Whatever!

CASS. What are your names?!

KARLA. I'm Karla!

GLEN. And I'm Glen!

CASS. Nice to meet you! I'm Cass! And this is Barbara!

BARBARA. She just bought my wig!

KARLA. It suits you!

CASS. Thank you!

GLEN. *(Referring to Lois.)* Who's that?!

CASS. That's my friend Lois!

GLEN. Doris?!

CASS. Lois!

LOIS. What?!

BARBARA. *(Refers to Lois and Cass.)* These two are nuts!

KARLA. Sluts?!

BARBARA. Nuts!

GLEN. Aren't these raincoats clammy?!

CASS. Yes!

GLEN. You can smell the other people who've worn them!

LOIS. That's true, but things are different in Brazil! *(They all look at Lois, perplexed.)*

CASS. Everyone ready for the Hurricane Deck?!

BARBARA. I know I am!

KARLA. You all go ahead! We'll catch up!

GLEN. We wanna get a couple pictures!

CASS. Okay! *(Glen snaps a couple of photos. Cass, Lois and Barbara head up and out. Once they're out of earshot, Karla's manner changes.)*

KARLA. *(Swatting at Glen's camera.)* All right, cut that out! They're gone!

GLEN. You think that was her?!

KARLA. It's hard to tell! I think so! *(Takes a cell phone out of her raincoat and dials a number.)*

GLEN. How did I do?! Did it seem genuine?!

KARLA. You were pushing it with the raincoat stuff!

GLEN. I was making conversation!

KARLA. Well, make less of it next time!

GLEN. You got it! Thanks for the feedback!

KARLA. *(Yells into the phone.)* I think we've found her! She's in Niagara Falls! … *Niagara Falls!* … The *waterfall!* … Yes! … We'll keep an eye on her and let you know for sure! … We'll keep an eye on her! … An *eye* on her! … An *eye!* … *Eye!* … An *eyeball!* … We'll call you back! *(Blackout.)*

Scene 6

Lights up inside the control room of the Maid of the Mist. *Captain Mike mans the wheel. Cass stands next to him in a blue disposable rain poncho, still wearing her wig, taking in the sights. We hear The Falls far off. Captain Mike speaks into a P.A. system while he steers the ship.*

CAPTAIN MIKE. *(Into the mike.)* And this boat got its name from an Indian princess, who was sent over The Falls in a canoe as a sacrifice to the thunder god, Hinum. And some believe her spirit still roams the caves behind The Falls. *(Mysteriously.)* The Maid of the Mist. *(Clicks off mike. and turns to Cass.)* It's spooky if I say it like that. Makes the trip more enjoyable.

CASS. Yes, you're quite the showman.

CAPTAIN MIKE. Thanks. You should know, by the way, I'm sort of bending the rules, letting you in the wheelhouse like this.

CASS. I appreciate it.

CAPTAIN MIKE. Figured you deserved special treatment. Most passengers don't stay on the boat five times in a row.

CASS. I was getting up the nerve to talk to you.

CAPTAIN MIKE. Really?

CASS. Yeah, I saw you from the Hurricane Deck, and I was telling my friend how I wanted to have sex with you.

CAPTAIN MIKE. Oh.

CASS. That's my friend down there. The one vomiting on deck. She's an alcoholic. *(Waves happily to Lois, then notices a lever.)* Hey, what's this do? *(She pulls the lever. A loud foghorn sounds.)*

CAPTAIN MIKE. Can you not pull things while you're up here?

CASS. Sorry. It's the new me. I'm taking the bull by the horns!

CAPTAIN MIKE. Olé.

CASS. Oh, you speak Spanish.

CAPTAIN MIKE. No.

CASS. I find Latino men so handsome. Or as your people say, "muy muy guapo."

CAPTAIN MIKE. I don't speak Spanish.

CASS. And I don't speak Swedish. *Yet.* Life is so full of possibilities. Do you find me attractive?

CAPTAIN MIKE. Sure.

CASS. You're such a flirt! Are you trying seduce me, you sailor boy, you?

CAPTAIN MIKE. No.

CASS. Why not? Aren't I pretty enough?

CAPTAIN MIKE. No, you're very pretty, I just —

CASS. It's the wig, isn't it? The humidity makes it frizz. *(Takes wig off.)*

CAPTAIN MIKE. I notice you're wearing a wedding ring.

CASS. Oh, this? No, this is just … I *found* this. I was camping in the desert and setting up a tent and there it was. This is nothing. *(Throws open the door behind her.)* Hey everybody! Free ring! *(Outside, the crowd cheers. Cass tosses the ring to them and slams the door shut.)* All gone.

CAPTAIN MIKE. You're kinda all over the place, aren't ya?

CASS. Yes. I used to speak lucidly. My thoughts used to connect with each other. But someone disappointed me in unspeakable ways, and now my synapses don't work all the way.

CAPTAIN MIKE. Was it your husband?

CASS. What?

CAPTAIN MIKE. Who disappointed you.

CASS. No, I don't have a husband.

CAPTAIN MIKE. Ah. Excuse me. *(Clicks on mike and speaks into it.)* In 1859, a French tightrope walker named Blondin went across The Falls on a three-inch-thick rope, with his terrified manager on his shoulders. Among the spectators was King Edward VII, who said afterwards "Thank God it is over! Please never attempt it again." *(Clicks mike off.)* So what do you do in real life?

CASS. I'm a ninth-grade math teacher.

CAPTAIN MIKE. Oh, a marm.

CASS. What?

CAPTAIN MIKE. A schoolmarm.

CASS. No, I *teach math*.

CAPTAIN MIKE. No, I know. And what's your husband do?

CASS. I said I don't have a — Are you trying to trick me?

CAPTAIN MIKE. *I* was married once.

CASS. Were you?

CAPTAIN MIKE. Her name was Dinah. She had a cotton candy cart up by the wax museum. The sweetest woman alive. We met bowling. Her hair was all up in this lump, with a pencil holding it together. You ever see that?

CASS. Sure.

CAPTAIN MIKE. I used to call her Lumpy. It was a nickname.

CASS. Cute.

CAPTAIN MIKE. Yeah, she was something.

CASS. Until she turned on you, right? Until she transformed into a grotesque stranger?

CAPTAIN MIKE. No. That never happened.

CASS. Oh. I assumed because you said "*was*" married.

CAPTAIN MIKE. No, we ... uh ... oh, never mind.

CASS. No, go ahead.

CAPTAIN MIKE. Well, you know those wholesale warehouse stores? You become a member and get huge amounts of food for pennies?

CASS. *Love* the Costco. You can buy a twenty-pound bag of Cheetos for four dollars.

CAPTAIN MIKE. Exactly. Well, I enjoyed shopping at Costco, but Dinah thought it was silly. Said the food was just too darn big.

21

CASS. So you divorced?

CAPTAIN MIKE. No. I came home late from The Falls one night, and the house was so quiet. Like cathedral quiet. Has your house ever been so quiet you thought you might stop breathing?

CASS. Yes. I've lived with that for years.

CAPTAIN MIKE. And I go to the kitchen, and Dinah is lying on the floor, and there's a restaurant-size four-gallon jar of peanut butter smeared across the tiles. She was apparently putting the jar away — it was kept on one of the higher shelves — and she lost her grip, and the peanut butter plummeted and smashed against her forehead. The coroner said that the weight of the blow could've killed a gorilla. She died nearly instantly.

CASS. My goodness.

CAPTAIN MIKE. I don't know why I was so stubborn. We didn't need all that peanut butter. A small jar would've been plenty. She must've gotten hungry waiting for me. And the thing is, I stopped to rent a video on the way home. And I think if I had just been a little earlier, or if I hadn't stopped for the video, maybe she wouldn't have reached for that gargantuan jar.

CASS. What video was it?

CAPTAIN MIKE. What?

CASS. What video? What'd you rent?

CAPTAIN MIKE. Uh … I think it was … *Caddyshack*.

CASS. Oh, that's good. That's a good movie.

CAPTAIN MIKE. I guess.

CASS. Sure. With the gopher and everything? That's funny.

CAPTAIN MIKE. Well, I didn't actually get to watch it.

CASS. Oh, that's right. I'm sorry. Oh my God, I'm so sorry. My husband's right, I'm such a scatterbrain.

CAPTAIN MIKE. Husband?

CASS. Did I say husband? I meant *houseboy*. I have a number of servants, and they're always teasing me, so … Husband, houseboy. See how they sound alike?

CAPTAIN MIKE. Excuse me. *(Clicks on mic and speaks into it.)* In 1911, Bobby Leach survived a plunge over The Falls in a cylindrical steel barrel. Years later, while vacationing in New Zealand, he slipped on an orange peel while walking down the street, developed complications, had his leg amputated, contracted gangrene poisoning and died. *(Clicks off mic.)*

CASS. *(Looking up at The Falls.)* Do many people survive?

CAPTAIN MIKE. The Falls? Some do. *I* did.

CASS. *(Beat.)* You didn't go over The Falls.

CAPTAIN MIKE. Sure I did. *(Refers to a crewman down on deck.)* Ask Pete down there. He'll tell ya.

CASS. Wow. You're like a daredevil.

CAPTAIN MIKE. I didn't even use a barrel.

CASS. Well that seems foolish.

CAPTAIN MIKE. I was pretty upset about Dinah.

CASS. *(Beat.)* Oh, I see.

CAPTAIN MIKE. It's hard to bounce back from something like that.

CASS. So you threw yourself in?

CAPTAIN MIKE. Yeah. I went over, I went under, and popped up downstream, bruised but kicking. Pete pulled me out. Go ask him.

CASS. I'm gonna.

CAPTAIN MIKE. Everything became clear after that. It was like God reached out and caught me, told me to keep going, don't lose faith. He gave me a sign.

CASS. Wow. That's what *I* need. Maybe not that holy-God-mumbo-jumbo, but a sign of some kind, something to believe in.

CAPTAIN MIKE. *(Beat.)* You wanna take the wheel for a few minutes?

CASS. Really? That doesn't seem dangerous to you?

CAPTAIN MIKE. We're in a smooth patch. I'll be right here.

CASS. All right then.

CAPTAIN MIKE. *(Putting her hands on wheel.)* Hands on ten and two.

CASS. *(Taking the wheel.)* Like this?

CAPTAIN MIKE. Uh-huh. *(Captain Mike stands close by, and occasionally helps her steer.)*

CASS. *(Steering.)* Wow. This is … How am I doing?

CAPTAIN MIKE. Great. A little to the left. There you go.

CASS. This is quite an honor.

CAPTAIN MIKE. Cass?

CASS. Yes?

CAPTAIN MIKE. I really like you.

CASS. You do?

CAPTAIN MIKE. Yes. And I meet a lot of people on this boat, thousands. But the fact is I'm basically a very lonely man.

CASS. So am I. Not that man bit, but everything else.

CAPTAIN MIKE. And I haven't … *been* with someone since Dinah, so I'm completely out of practice, and I don't know how to say the right things. But if you meant what you said before, about … you know … I'd like to spend the night with you. I hope that isn't too forward.

CASS. Let's dock this dinghy. *(Pulls fog horn. Blackout.)*

Scene 7

The hotel room, littered with tiny empty liquor bottles. The barrel is out and upright. Lois is in the barrel, a shower cap on her head, drinking from a tiny bottle. Cass enters wearing big overalls.

CASS. Good mornin'!

LOIS. *(Toasts her with tiny bottle.)* L'chaim!

CASS. What are you doing?

LOIS. I'm scraping the bottom of my barrel! *(Laughs drunkenly.)*

CASS. I'm famished. How 'bout you? *(Goes to phone and dials room service.)*

LOIS. I didn't know where you went. You left without me.

CASS. *(Into the phone.)* I'd like a quart of OJ and a stack of flap-jacks … Room 232. Thanks. *(Hangs up.)*

LOIS. I searched that boat from top to bottom. I thought you might've fallen overboard.

CASS. I spent the night with the captain.

LOIS. Tramp.

CASS. You wouldn't *believe* the things I checked off my list.

LOIS. Good God, I don't wanna know.

24

CASS. You drank all this liquor?

LOIS. Aren't the bottles cute? Everything's so little around here. Little and drinkable.

CASS. Get out of the barrel, you look like a rodeo clown.

LOIS. This hat came free with the room! Free hats, free soap and itty-bitty bottles of hooch!

CASS. *(Motioning her out of the barrel.)* Let's go.

LOIS. Don't ever leave me like that again.

CASS. I came back.

LOIS. When you *felt* like it! You came back when it was good for you!

CASS. Are you mad at me?

LOIS. You said you had my back! But you obviously don't give a *shit* about me! That's all right. I don't need you. I don't need anybody! Just my barrel. *(Ducks down into barrel.)*

CASS. *(Peeking into barrel.)* Hey, you saw my list. I'm on a spree. I gotta grab what I can. I *had* to go with the captain.

LOIS. *(Inside barrel.)* Is he your new *sidekick*?

CASS. No ma'am. That position's been filled. *(Beat.)* I'm sorry I left you alone.

LOIS. *(Peeks up.)* I lost my watch.

CASS. What watch?

LOIS. My honeymoon watch. Ted bought it for me when we got married. It was engraved. "Love Always" it said and I lost it.

CASS. When? Today?

LOIS. No. On our honeymoon.

CASS. Well that was a long time ago. I'm sure he's forgiven you.

LOIS. Nope, he was pissed. Still mentions it every once in a while. I was drunk. And I was leaning over the railing, and it just slipped off. It disappeared into the mist of The Falls, just like *I'm* gonna do.

CASS. Hey, enough of that talk.

LOIS. But Ted and I were happy once. And then that watch fell off, and he's hated me ever since.

CASS. I'm sure he doesn't hate you. Call him up and *ask* him if he hates you.

LOIS. No, he's done with me. He said so in his letter. "Dearest Boozehound, I am done with you." *(Beat.)* You're not done with

25

me, are you?

CASS. Of course not. We have a helicopter ride scheduled, remember? *(Lois nods. There's a knock at the door.)*

LOIS. I hope that's room service.

CASS. Come in. *(Lois gets out of the barrel as Captain Mike enters with a box of groceries.)* Captain Mike was unloading the car.

LOIS. Ahoy, Captain!

CAPTAIN MIKE. Good morning ... uh ...

CASS. Lois.

CAPTAIN MIKE. Right.

CASS. She's the alcoholic I was telling you about.

LOIS. I'm sorry I got sick on your boat, Cap'n.

CAPTAIN MIKE. It's a common reaction to the awesome splendor of Mother Nature.

LOIS. I think it was the tequila actually.

CASS. *(To Lois.)* Wanna see what we got?

CAPTAIN MIKE. We went to Costco. *(Cass pulls an enormous can of Spaghettios out of the bag.)*

CASS. Look at this.

LOIS. Wow.

CASS. *(Tosses giant bag of Cheetos to Lois.)* Try these.

LOIS. *(Overwhelmed by bag of Cheetos.)* Help, I'm shrinking. *(Holds up Cheetos and tiny bottle respectively.)* Eat me. Drink me. Eat me. Drink me.

CAPTAIN MIKE. Is that a barrel?

LOIS. What?

CAPTAIN MIKE. Because, you know, I don't want to make assumptions here, and I don't know what your plans are, but going over The Falls in a barrel is against the law. You know that, right? And as a member of the Niagara Falls family and its affiliated companies —

LOIS. No, this isn't a barrel. It's ... my bed. I sleep here. I have back problems. Some people sleep on boards. I sleep in a barrel.

CAPTAIN MIKE. I see.

LOIS. Time to make my bed! *(Drags barrel into the bathroom.)*

CASS. Isn't she funny?

CAPTAIN MIKE. I'm gonna have to send somebody to pick up that barrel.

CASS. Hey, *you* went over.

CAPTAIN MIKE. And I was arrested. The law is the law. I can't let her —

CASS. She won't actually *do* it.

CAPTAIN MIKE. How do you know? Alcoholics are an irrational bunch.

CASS. I've made it my job. Since I couldn't save my mother. *(Beat.)* I know that doesn't make any sense but ... leave her barrel alone, okay?

CAPTAIN MIKE. *(Pause.)* Okay. I'm such a softy. I should head in. I have a ten A.M. tour.

CASS. Thanks for carrying the food up.

CAPTAIN MIKE. Sure. Thank you for ... everything.

CASS. Oh, go on, shy boy.

CAPTAIN MIKE. Can I see you tonight?

CASS. No, you can't.

CAPTAIN MIKE. Why not?

CASS. I had fun. But ... I'm here to experience as much as I can.

CAPTAIN MIKE. We'll do something different.

CASS. Right, but I have this whole list. See? So much to do. *(Holds up list.)* And "Torrid fling" is checked off.

CAPTAIN MIKE. Oh. I didn't realize I was part of a scavenger hunt.

CASS. Now don't get all hurt. I have seven years of mistakes to correct, so cut me some slack.

CAPTAIN MIKE. I was only proposing dinner.

CASS. *(Beat.)* Well ... hold on, let me see what I can do. *(Flips through her list.)* Uhh ... no ... *no* ... Wait, I might have something here. Where were you seven years ago?

CAPTAIN MIKE. Seven years ago?

CASS. April twenty-sixth.

CAPTAIN MIKE. *(Trying to remember.)* Gosh, I guess ... if it was April, then ... I would've been working the check-in desk at the Hilton.

CASS. Oh.

CAPTAIN MIKE. Is that something you can work with?

CASS. Uhh, yeah. That's *good*. It's a long shot but ...

CAPTAIN MIKE. What is it?

27

CASS. Nothing. We'll have dinner, okay?

CAPTAIN MIKE. Okay.

LOIS. *(Entering.)* The bed's all made.

CASS. Lois, Captain Mike is gonna overlook that barrel, but you better make sure no one sees it, otherwise you're gonna get us all in trouble. Now keep it under wraps or he'll take it away.

LOIS. Fine.

CASS. I'm gonna walk the captain to his car.

LOIS. Hurry back. *(Captain Mike and Cass exit. Lois sits alone for a couple beats, then makes her way to the phone and dials. Into the phone.)* Hi Willy, it's me. Is Ted there? … Ted, your brother. Don't play dumb, Willy, I know he's staying with you. Put him on … Is that what he told you to say? … I just want to ask him something … Yes he *is* there! You're a goddamn liar! *(Slams down phone. Lois collects herself. Then she runs into the bathroom and drags the barrel out. She's heading for the door when someone knocks. Lois freezes. She looks at her barrel and panics. She starts to roll it into the bathroom. Another knock. There's no time. Lois throws a blanket over the barrel and leaves it where it is. Another knock. She runs into the closet to hide. A key turns in the lock, Karla peeks in and looks around, then she and Glen enter in stolen bellhop uniforms.)*

KARLA. It's clear. Look around. Be quick. *(Glen and Karla search the room.)*

GLEN. This place reeks of booze.

KARLA. *(Speaks into a handheld tape recorder.)* Seedy hotel. Signs of debauchery.

GLEN. *(Finds giant can of Spaghettios.)* Look at this.

KARLA. Put it away. We're looking for an I.D., something with her name on it. He wanted proof.

GLEN. *(Lifts blanket.)* Hey, looky-loo!

KARLA. *(Into the tape recorder.)* One large wooden barrel. *(Lois suddenly leaps out of the closet with an iron. They all scream.)*

LOIS, GLEN and KARLA. Ahhhhhhhhhh!

GLEN.	KARLA.
Mother of Pearl!	Where'd she come from?!

LOIS. *(Waving the iron.)* No one is taking that barrel!

GLEN	KARLA
Lady, I've had bypass surgery!	Now hold on a second!

Whaddaya tryin' to do?   Nobody wants your barrel!

LOIS. Hey, you're that couple.

KARLA. That's right. You *know* us. Now put the iron down.

LOIS. What are you doing here?

KARLA. We ... work for the hotel. Been here for years.

GLEN. We're bellhops.

LOIS. I thought you were honeymooners.

KARLA. We are. We couldn't afford to take the time off.

GLEN. We're very poor.

KARLA. So we honeymoon during our breaks.

GLEN. What better place, right?

LOIS. That's screwy.

KARLA. Yeah, well.

LOIS. Huh. All right then. *(Puts iron down.)* So where's our flap-jacks?

GLEN. Flapjacks?

LOIS. Don't tell me you forgot them. We ordered room service *ages* ago. Well, no tip for you! You are the *suckiest* bellhops I've ever met! No wonder you're so poor. *(Beat.)* So what are you doing here then?

GLEN. Oh we ... uh ...

KARLA. We have some questions for you. A guest evaluation. We want to make sure you're comfortable.

LOIS. Well, I don't have time to fill out questionnaires.

KARLA. It's oral. It'll just take a sec. Glen will tidy up while we do it. *(It takes him a moment, but Glen understands. He goes back to searching, while he pretends to clean.)*

LOIS. I got a lot to accomplish today. I can't —

KARLA. *(Flips open notebook and takes notes.)* Your name?

LOIS. Lois Coleman. Aren't you kinda old to be bellhops?

GLEN. They're real liberal here.

KARLA. Point of departure?

LOIS. Port Authority.

KARLA. Anyone else staying in this room?

LOIS. Cass. We took the bus up together.

KARLA. Uh-huh. And do you find our facilities up to your expectations?

LOIS. Your *gift* shop sucks.

KARLA. Why's that?

29

CASS. So what?

KIP. I hired those people.

CASS. See, it's always about you, Kip. What *you* did. What *you* want.

LOIS. What *you* swallowed.

CASS. Lois …

LOIS. I'm sorry. I'll just read one of these poems. *(Grabs Neruda book.)*

KIP. Is it because I'm not aggressive enough? I can change. I can be more butch.

CASS. I don't want you to be butch. *(Kip grabs Cass suddenly and tries to drag her out the door.)*

KIP. Fuck you, you bitch! You're coming with me, or I'll kick the shit out of you. *(Cass squirms out of his arms and slaps him hard across the face.)*

CASS. What the hell's the matter with you?

KIP. *(Collapses, sobbing.)* I'm sorry! Okay?! What else do I need to do? Just tell me, and I'll do it. I know I was dishonest. I know you're disappointed, but give me another chance.

CASS. Kip, you're embarrassing me. Pull yourself together. *(There is a knock at the door. No one moves. There is another knock.)*

LOIS. I'll get it. *(Lois goes to door and opens it. Captain Mike is standing there. He looks down at Kip and back up at Cass.)*

CAPTAIN MIKE. Hi. Are we … still on for dinner?

CASS. *(Brightly.)* Sure. Just a sec.

CAPTAIN MIKE. Who's this?

CASS. Uh, this is Kip. My houseboy. He's upset because I've cut his wages.

CAPTAIN MIKE. Huh. *(Turns to Kip.)* Nice to meet you. I'm Captain Mike.

KIP. Oh, a military man.

CAPTAIN MIKE. Not exactly. That's a nice sweater.

LOIS. I hear he's got drawers filled with sweaters, eh Kipper?

CAPTAIN MIKE. I'm a sweater man myself. This one I'm wearing —

KIP. It's nice.

CAPTAIN MIKE. Thanks. Bought it from a lady across the street from me. Her name's Melba. She runs a little business making sweaters year round. Does great work. I'll give you the address.

KIP. I'd appreciate that.

CASS. Okay, that's enough. What'd I tell you about bothering the guests, houseboy? Go dust my boudoir.

CAPTAIN MIKE. He wasn't bothering me.

CASS. Can you wait outside? I'll be with you in a bit.

CAPTAIN MIKE. Well, okay. I'll … I'll be down in the car. *(Exits.)*

KIP. I thought there might be another man. This explains everything.

CASS. I just met him.

KIP. Did you sleep with him? *(No response.)* You *did!* You slept with him!

CASS. Excuse me! *(Whips out doll head and shakes it at him.)* *Excuuuuuse* me!

KIP. I was wondering where Vivian went. *(Off Cass' look.)* I wanted to dispose of her. As I did the others.

CASS. Take it. She scares my friends. *(Tosses Barbie head at him.)* Go home, Kip. You're wasting your time here. *(To Lois.)* And you, don't do anything ridiculous. I'm coming back. Do you understand that I'm coming back? *(Lois nods.)* All right then. Goodbye. *(Exits.)*

LOIS. *(Pause.)* Well, at least you tried. It's nice you came all this way with that box.

KIP. She didn't even care.

LOIS. She's a new person now.

KIP. But I worked so hard at finding her.

LOIS. I would've taken you back. If you were my husband and you tracked me down, I would've gone home and made a real commitment to start over.

KIP. I'll get her back.

LOIS. Someday maybe.

KIP. I love her. It's like … she doesn't know that anymore.

LOIS. No, she knows. She just doesn't care. *(Lights fade on Kip and Lois.)*

41

Scene 2

Lights up on a medieval restaurant. Cass and Captain Mike are dressed in flowing medieval garb. Medieval music plays.

CASS. I've never eaten at one of these places.

CAPTAIN MIKE. Different, right? Unique? It's called the Medieval Manor.

CASS. I didn't know they made you wear these clothes.

CAPTAIN MIKE. A jester comes around during dessert. And later, they have a jousting show.

CASS. Fun. *(A waitress dressed as a serving wench approaches. She speaks in a Cockney accent.)*

WAITRESS #1. 'Ello folks. My name is Mary Pickerling, and I'll be your scullery maid this evenin'. Can I get ye two a mug of mead?

CAPTAIN MIKE. Not right now, thank you.

WAITRESS #1. Very well, Guv'nuh. 'Ere's the menus, and I'll be back to talk about ye olde specials. *(Hands them menus and then exits.)*

CASS. She seems like a saucy wench.

CAPTAIN MIKE. Yes she does. So you like it here, right? I'm trying to jazz things up a bit. Some new experiences for mi'lady.

CASS. I can see that. I'm checking off "Wear velvet." *(Pulls out list. Lights down on them, and up on a restaurant decorated in Native American décor. We hear drums playing quietly. Karla is alone at a table. Lois staggers in drunk, yelling over her shoulder.)*

LOIS. Well, go screw a monkey, ya shit-eating bastard! *(Sees Karla.)* Oh hello, Miss Marple. You mind if I sit?

KARLA. This is my alone time actually.

LOIS. *(Plops down.)* That whoreson at the bar cut me off. Said I had to order some food. So whaddaya recommend?

KARLA. I recommend you sit somewhere else.

LOIS. *(Flips through upside down menu.)* What is this? Where the hell am I? *(A waitress approaches dressed as a Native American.)*

WAITRESS #2. How. Welcome to The Reservation. I'll be your serving squaw. My name is Walks-with-a-Tray. Can I take your order?

KARLA. I'll have the buffalo burger with a side of maize.

WAITRESS #2. *(To Lois.)* And for you, pale-face?

LOIS. Has anyone ever boycotted this place?

WAITRESS #2. May I interest you in the Powwow Platter?

LOIS. This is terribly offensive. You're not even Native American.

WAITRESS #2. You wanna order or picket?

LOIS. I bet you're an actress. You've got that bitter edge, like waiting on me is so beneath you when you should be a great big star by now.

WAITRESS #2. Lady, I've got a six-top sending me smoke signals. I'll come back when you're ready to order. *(Walks off.)*

LOIS. Hey, Meryl Streep! Bring me the Clams Casino, and then do a little monologue for me! *(Lights down on them, and up on Glen and Kip at a Gothic theme restaurant. We hear rattling chains, ghost sounds and other haunted house noises. Kip hands Glen an envelope filled with cash.)*

KIP. There you go. It's all there. You can count it if you want.

GLEN. *(Counts the money.)* I promised Karla I would. She gave me real strict instructions. Not that we don't trust you or anything.

KIP. *(Peruses a menu.)* You did a great job tracking her down.

GLEN. Oh, thanks. Karla says I need to concentrate more, make sure I take my meds in the mornin'. Don't ya love this place? I eat here two or three times a week. Kinda cheesy but it makes me chuckle. *(A waitress dressed as a vampiress approaches. She carries a large scythe and speaks in a Transylvanian accent.)*

WAITRESS #3. Carpe Noctem, and velcome to the Maison de Macabre. I am Gormina Gallows. May I refresh your Diet Pepsis?

KIP. I'm ready to order actually.

WAITRESS #3. Yes, my liege.

KIP. I'll have the Grave-Robber Nachos.

GLEN. And I'll have the Chicken Wrap of Doom.

WAITRESS #3. Horrifically good choices. *(She lets out a blood-curdling scream, startling the men, then exits with a flip of her cape.)*

KIP. That was unnecessary.

GLEN. Yeah, she does that. *(Puts envelope away.)* Thanks for the dough. Six or seven more gigs like this, and we'll be able to move out of that youth hostel.

KIP. Turns out it was money down the tube. Cass didn't take me back.

GLEN. No? Aw well, she'll come around. They usually do. Karla did, mostly. And there's no way you did worse than I did.

KIP. Wanna bet?

GLEN. Two years ago, I had an affair.

KIP. Shitting Barbie heads turns me on.

GLEN. *(Beat.)* Okay, you win. *(Lights down on them, and up on Medieval Manor. Waitress #1 enters and serves an enormous tray of food.)*

WAITRESS #1. For the Guv'nuh we've got a roasted pig on a spit, and for the Duchess we've got the venison-chicken combo.

CASS. *(Holds up enormous chicken leg.)* Look at me, I'm Henry the Eighth!

WAITRESS #1. *(She's seen this a million times.)* Oh I've never seen *that* before. *(Walks off.)*

CASS. I'm so glad you brought me here. I've checked off six items already.

CAPTAIN MIKE. I thought it might be up your alley.

CASS. And look at these portions! To think of all those Pasta Thursdays with Kip when I could've been eating savory meat pies with you.

CAPTAIN MIKE. Oh, he's a cook *and* a houseboy?

CASS. As a matter of fact, he is. But let's not talk about Kip, okay?

CAPTAIN MIKE. Okay. *(They go back to eating. Cass seems distracted. After a couple beats she asks …)*

CASS. How do you know what to *do?*

CAPTAIN MIKE. Do?

CASS. Yeah, just … *everything.* How do you even know what socks to put on in the morning when the color alone could change your destiny?

CAPTAIN MIKE. I guess I don't really think about that when I'm getting dressed.

CASS. No? What do you think about?

CAPTAIN MIKE. Breakfast mostly.

CASS. *(Beat.)* I used to think about breakfast. I *loved* breakfast. Darn that Kip and his secrets.

CAPTAIN MIKE. I thought we weren't talking about him.

CASS. Right. *(Beat.)* You think I'm insane, don't you?

CAPTAIN MIKE. No, I think you're … effervescent.

CASS. *(Lights up.)* Like sparkling cider?!

CAPTAIN MIKE. Sure. *(Cass throws herself into his arms. They disappear under the table, kissing. Lights out on them, up on Lois and Karla. Lois prattles on drunkenly.)*

LOIS. And Ted was *obsessed* with Egyptian history, which I personally found to be a big giant yawn. Every year he'd say, "Let's go see the pyramids, let's go see the pyramids."

KARLA. Where the hell's that Indian with my food?

LOIS. Well there was no way I was spending the only two weeks of vacation we got, in the middle of a desert looking at sand and busted statues. So we'd go to Napa Valley instead, because that's what *I* wanted. I think that got to him. *(Waitress #2 rushes by.)*

KARLA. Hey Pocahontas, d'you forget my burger?

WAITRESS #2. Two minutes. Me take-um smoke break.

KARLA. Damn Injuns. I'm outta here.

LOIS. Wait, I wanna hire you.

KARLA. Hire me? For what?

LOIS. My friend Cass, she's a real sweet lady, but she distracts me. I shoulda been dead two days ago. I was thinking maybe you could make sure I go through with it.

KARLA. That'd cost ya.

LOIS. Whatever it takes. So long as you answer a question.

KARLA. It's your dime.

LOIS. How'd you do it? With everything that happens between two people, how'd you manage to stay married for thirty-eight years? *(Lights up on Glen and Kip.)*

GLEN. We've had a lot of therapy. If you need someone to salvage your marriage, you should see our counselor. She single-handedly pulled Karla and me back from the abyss. *(The lights go up and down on Karla and Glen respectively for the rest of the scene.)*

KARLA. I don't even think about my marriage anymore. Why this, why that? I have no idea how it works, and that's fine by me. It's like Stonehenge, an unknowable mystery the world has come to accept.

GLEN. The affair was a mistake. But my God that woman was beautiful. She had this little business knitting sweaters, so she got her supplies from us. Her name was Melba.

KIP. Melba?

GLEN. And one day, she just whispered her address into my ear. That's how it started.

KARLA. I was doing the laundry and I found an address in his pants pocket. And I marched upstairs and said, "What is this?" And he said: "Just some litter I picked up. Doin' a good deed."

GLEN. I'm not a very good liar.

KARLA. I had sensed something for weeks.

GLEN. She had the craziest look in her eye.

KARLA. Finally I had proof.

GLEN. She hopped in the car and drove to the address.

KARLA. You really meant that suicide threat, right?

LOIS. You betcha.

KARLA. Good. Because what I'm about to tell you, take it to the grave.

GLEN. My fours look like nines sometimes. My penmanship has never been very good. And my fours look like nines. That's what happened. The address was 2-1-4 Windermere Drive, and she snuck into 2-1-9 Windermere Drive.

KARLA. The woman didn't hear me come in. She was a lot younger than I imagined. Pretty. She was in the kitchen, wearing a little slip, her hair all up in this lump, making herself a peanut butter sandwich.

GLEN. There was an extraordinarily large jar, which Karla raised over her head. She says she was just gonna threaten her with it.

KARLA. I lost my grip. I yelled something. "You retarded whore!" or something like that, and I lost my grip. Really, I didn't mean for it to … Gosh she looked surprised.

GLEN. She came home and told me how she lost her grip while threatening my mistress at 2-1-9 Windermere Drive.

KARLA. He said she lived at 2-1-4, not 2-1-9.

GLEN. Gosh she looked surprised.

KARLA. It was pretty tense for a few months.

GLEN. I broke it off with Melba.

KARLA. But no one ever came looking for me. Like there wasn't even an investigation. Odd, right? Ya gotta love the Buffalo police force.

46

GLEN. But I think it's gonna come back, you know? Those things usually do. So really, we're kinda watching our backs until it does. *(Waitress #3 lets out another blood-curdling scream, and slams down the check.)*
WAITRESS #3. You can pay in the morgue! *(Blackout.)*

Scene 3

Lights up on hotel room. Cass and Captain Mike enter after a long night out. They're still wearing their crowns from dinner.

CAPTAIN MIKE. There you go. An official escort home.
CASS. That really wasn't necessary, Captain.
CAPTAIN MIKE. Cass … I have a proposal.
CASS. Oh, you do? Well, lay it on me.
CAPTAIN MIKE. I was thinking we could maybe travel the country together. Get a motor home, and roam from state to state. Like gypsies.
CASS. Gypsies?
CAPTAIN MIKE. Yeah. You'll see something new every day. We'll work down that list of yours. Whaddaya say?
CASS. *(Beat.)* I *knew* it. You *are* the man I was supposed to meet seven years ago! What are the odds?!
CAPTAIN MIKE. What do you mean seven years ago?
CASS. You worked at the Hilton. I had reservations. If Kip hadn't proposed, I would've met you. Heck, we'd probably have a couple kids by now. But like they say, it's never too late.
CAPTAIN MIKE. I was already married.
CASS. What?
CAPTAIN MIKE. Seven years ago. Lumpy and I were already married when I was at the Hilton. Nothing would've happened between us back then. I loved my wife very much.
CASS. Oh. Right.
CAPTAIN MIKE. But who cares about seven years ago? The here

47

and now's what's important. Whaddaya say? A Winnebago? The open road?

CASS. *(Pause.)* No, I don't think I can do that.

CAPTAIN MIKE. Why not?

CASS. My list. I can't just run off. I haven't gone parachuting yet, or learned how to spin plates on sticks or —

CAPTAIN MIKE. Right, what I'm saying is we can do all those things *together*. I've never gone parachuting either.

CASS. Plus I'm worried about Lois. I can't just —

CAPTAIN MIKE. She can come too.

CASS. Captain … I hardly even know you. *(Beat.)* I'm sorry. I can't go.

CAPTAIN MIKE. *(Pause.)* This is about that houseboy, isn't it?

CASS. Now look here, my domestics are no concern of yours.

CAPTAIN MIKE. Do you still love him?

CASS. My God, first Kip, then Lois, and now — Why is everyone I know so damn clingy?

CAPTAIN MIKE. Maybe I should go.

CASS. I'm sorry. Your offers are wonderful. *(Beat.)* Am I tempted? Yes. Are you perfect? I think so. But so was Kip. And you'll change just like he did. One day I'll turn around, and you'll be a troll. And the world'll turn upside down, and where'll that leave me? On my crown, that's where. Why can't people just be who you want them to be? *(Silence. Then a key turns in the lock and Glen, in his stolen bellhop uniform and carrying a covered platter, enters with Kip.)*

KIP. Thank god, she's here.

GLEN. *(Puts down platter.)* I told you I'd get you in.

CASS. Kip, what are you doing? You can't just let yourself in here.

KIP. We need to talk.

CASS. I'm not allowed to talk to strangers.

KIP. You can fuck 'em though, right?

CAPTAIN MIKE. I should probably leave you two alone.

CASS. Please don't.

KIP. I'm sorry. Scratch that fuck comment. It slipped out. What I meant to say is I love you.

CASS. Go away.

KIP. I can't. Glen here called his marriage counselor on our behalf.

48

CAPTAIN MIKE. So you *are* married.

CASS. Captain —

KIP. Yes, we are.

CASS. Kip — !

KIP. Glen says this therapist is a miracle worker.

CASS. Well that's swell, but I'm not a blind deaf mute.

KIP. Just give it a chance. She's at the hospital doing some volunteer work —

GLEN. For the kids. She's real generous.

KIP. But she said she'd get here ASAP.

CASS. Get here? This is *my* room! You can't just invite people over!

GLEN. Karla was resistant at first too.

CASS. Okay Kip, you need to quit it now, because the captain and I are buying a Winnebago.

CAPTAIN MIKE. We are?

CASS. Yes. I changed my mind. I wanna go now.

CAPTAIN MIKE. I think you just want to run away again.

CASS. No, I don't, I — I wanna be with you. You said you'd parachute with me. This has nothing to do with Kip. *(To Kip.)* You see what you're doing?

KIP. *I'll* go parachuting.

CASS. You had your chance. *(To Captain Mike.)* Now come on, let's get that motor home.

CAPTAIN MIKE. No. That was selfish of me to propose. I was pretty sure he was your husband.

CASS. So what?!

CAPTAIN MIKE. I think you and Kip should sort this out first.

CASS. Forget about Kip. *I* have. It's easy. Watch. *(She pretends to forget Kip.)* See? No Kip. He's forgotten.

CAPTAIN MIKE. He's not a wig, Cass. You can't just cross him off your list.

KIP. That's right.

CASS. *(Beat.)* Okay, there's some serious double-teaming going on here, which I really don't appreciate. *(Cass backs to the door, but Glen is blocking it. He pulls out a gun and points it at her.)*

GLEN. I'm sorry, you're not allowed to leave.

CASS. What is going *on?!*

(Janie reads from a list, and takes notes. The questions are fairly rapid-fire.) My partner loves me. *(Everyone except Captain Mike raises a hand.)* My partner is attractive. *(Everyone except Captain Mike raises a hand.)* My partner works hard. *(Everyone except Captain Mike raises a hand.)* My partner has a drinking problem. *(Only Captain Mike raises his hand.)* Good. My partner is dishonest. *(Cass, Karla, Captain Mike raise a hand.)* My partner sometimes frightens me. *(Cass, Glen and Captain Mike raise a hand.)* My partner and I can talk openly about our sexual fears, preferences and dislikes. *(Karla, Glen, Lois and Captain Mike, with a nudge from Lois, raise a hand.)* Great. I don't like my partner's choice of friends. *(Kip raises his hand.)* I don't like my partner's choice of hobbies. *(Cass raises her hand.)* My partner is holding me back. *(Cass raises her hand.)* My partner has made me vomit. *(Cass raises her hand.)* I love my partner. *(Everyone raises a hand.)* I hate my partner. *(Everyone raises a hand.)* I want security. *(Everyone raises a hand.)* I want unconditional love. *(Everyone raises a hand.)* I want my partner to change. *(Everyone raises a hand.)* I want to travel. *(Cass and Captain Mike raise a hand.)* I want children. *(Cass and Captain Mike raise a hand.)* My partner is not the person I married. *(Cass and Captain Mike raise a hand.)* The capital of Minnesota is Duluth. *(Pause. They all look at each other nervously. Glen tentatively raises his hand.)* Interesting. Let me just tally up the results. *(Janie whips out an abacus and does some "tallying.")*

LOIS. I took that same test last month in *Cosmo.*

JANIE. *(Adding on abacus.)* Did you score as poorly then? Because according to my calculations, you and your husband are virtual strangers. *(Tosses abacus aside.)* Everyone else gets a gold star. *(She honks a bike horn.)*

KIP. *(To Cass.)* See that? Gold star. That means we're good together.

JANIE. No it doesn't. It's too early to determine who does and doesn't belong together. First I have to find out how well you know each other. And in order to do that we need to play *The Newlywed Game.*

EVERYONE except KIP. *(Giddy overlapping.)* Oh, I love that game! Very good show! Bob Eubanks is quite the looker! The whoopie questions! They should bring that back! "In the butt, Bob!" Etc.

KIP. That's it! The whole thing is off! I don't like games! I don't like group therapy! And I don't like clowns! This is everything I don't like!

CASS. And everything I *do* like, Kip.

KIP. We can find another therapist.

CASS. I don't want another therapist! I want the clown! I'm sorry she's not what you had in mind, but sometimes that's what happens in life. You said you were willing to change. I guess that was another lie.

KIP. It wasn't.

CASS. If you want to call it off, then we're done. It's up to you.

KIP. *(Pause.)* Okay. Let's play the game.

JANIE. Wonderful! Honesty, assertion, concession! Another gold star! *(Honks her bike horn.)* Now I'm gonna pass out some questions, and I want you to write down the answers on these cards. No peeking at what your spouse writes. *(Passes out cue cards, markers and questions.)* And while you do that, I'm gonna tell an inspirational story. *(The couples get to work reading the questions and writing the answers on the large cards.)* Right after my husband Gary and I got married, we hit a bad patch. He was fucking a meter maid and I was sniffing wood glue. It was not a happy time. I felt betrayed and alone, so I bought a ticket on the *Maid of the Mist*, thinking I'd throw myself overboard. And there I was, on the boat, mist all around, The Falls thundering in front of me, and I thought, "Do it, Janie. Now's the time." And I lifted one leg over the railing, ready to end it all, when the most miraculous and unbelievable thing imaginable happened. *(The couples, who haven't really been listening, put down their markers, eager to play the game.)*

THE COUPLES. *(Giddy overlapping.)* All done! Ready! Finished! Let's play! You're goin' down! "In the butt, Bob!" *(Etc.)*

JANIE. *(Noticeably disappointed.)* Oh, well all right. You're all so quick. Guess I'll finish my story later. *(Janie pulls bells, whistles, buzzers and a couple of tape recorders out of her briefcase. She presses play and game-show music blares.)* Now remember, each question is worth twenty points. Question number one: Ladies, what is your husband's pet-name for you? We'll begin with Lois.

LOIS. Oh this is easy. Ted calls me this all the time. It's definitely, one hundred percent Stumble-Bum.

JANIE. Flip that card, Ted. *(He does. Buzzer. Then "Awwwww.")* He said Lushy.

LOIS. Lushy?!

CAPTAIN MIKE. Sorry, darling. We have *so many* pet names, it's hard to keep track.

JANIE. Cass?

CASS. Well there are a few, but mostly he calls me Lifesaver. *(Kip flips his card: "Lifesaver." Janie dings her bell. Applause from the tape recorder. Kip claps happily. Cass smiles.)*

KIP. Yes! Lifesaver it is!

JANIE. Which brings us to Karla.

KARLA. My answer is Josef Mengele. *(Glen flips his card. Bells ring.)*

JANIE. Josef Mengele! Very good. Question Number Two: What were the first words your husband ever spoke to you? Karla, we'll go back to you.

KARLA. Oh gee, that was so long ago. I think he said … "Is that your hashish pipe?" *(Glen flips his card.)*

JANIE. Glen wrote, "Are you *using* that hashish pipe?" Judges? *(Presses buzzer.)* Oh, so sorry. Choosing the right words: imperative to a happy marriage. Cass? Kip's first words to you?

CASS. I believe he said … "Help, help. I can't swim. Holy crap, I'm drowning." *(Kip flips card. Bells ring. Applause. Kip pumps his hand in victory. Cass is having fun.)*

JANIE. That's right! "Help-help-I-can't-swim-holy-crap-I'm-drowning!"

KIP. *(To Cass.)* And you said we were strangers.

CAPTAIN MIKE. Congratulations.

CASS. Thank you.

LOIS. *(To Captain Mike.)* Cut that out. *(To Janie.)* My husband has a wandering eye.

JANIE. And who can blame him? Ted's first words to you?

LOIS. "Don't worry, I know the Heimlich."

JANIE. And Ted says … *(Captain Mike flips the card.)*

CAPTAIN MIKE and JANIE. "Hey lady, you puked in my hat." *(Buzzer sounds.)*

JANIE. I'm sorry, that's incorrect, but now it's the husbands' turns. Let's see if you can make up some points. Kip, the name of the person your wife lost her virginity to.

KIP. His name better have been Kip, otherwise she has some serious explaining to do. *(Cass flips her card. Bells ring, applause.)*
JANIE. Kip is correct!
LOIS. Wow, that makes me sad and uncomfortable.
JANIE. Now Glen. Your wife lost her virginity to … ?
GLEN. Jackson Pollock! *(Karla flips her card. Bells. Applause.)*
JANIE. Correct! And finally, Ted's answer.
CAPTAIN MIKE. Uh … gosh, I don't know, I'll say … Dennis? *(Lois flips card. Ding-ding!)*
JANIE. Dennis is correct! *(Lois and Captain Mike exchange perplexed looks. That's weird.)* Okay, one question left, and it's a bonus question worth thirty-five points, so this is still anyone's game. *(Turns to Lois and Captain Mike.)* Except yours.
LOIS. It's certainly not my fault we're doing so poorly. Aside from that Dennis thing, my husband's an imbecile.
CAPTAIN MIKE. See, this is why I left her. On top of the drinking, there's the non-stop verbal abuse.
JANIE. Okay. Now tell *her* that, Ted. Go on. Face her and tell her what you feel. From the heart.
CAPTAIN MIKE. *(Turns and faces Lois.)* Lois, it hurts me when you insult and degrade me in front of your friends. I understand you have rage inside you, but it causes me pain when you aim it at me. I just want to help you and love you. *(Captain Mike faces front again. Lois seems confused and moved at the same time.)*
JANIE. Very nice. Let's see if it makes a difference in the final round. Ready? "If you had to describe your wife as a fairy tale character, which one would it be?" Glen?
GLEN. Well, because of her sweet tooth and extensive lederhosen collection, I'm gonna have to say … Gretel. *(Karla flips her card. Bells. Applause. Karla and Glen hug and clap, elated.)*
JANIE. Terrific. Bonus question to you, Ted.
CAPTAIN MIKE. Gosh, there could be a couple answers here. Tweedledee, Tweedledum. *(Lois smiles encouragingly.)* I'll say Tweedledee. *(Lois flips card. Buzzer.)*
JANIE. Awww. She said Thumbelina.
LOIS. That's okay. It was a good try, Ted.
CAPTAIN MIKE. Thank you.
JANIE. I sense some healing. I like that. And finally, we turn to

59

What point?

(Shows book.) On the map. The point of no return.

LOIS. Whaddaya mean, point of no — ?!

CASS. Hey, look at the kids at the picnic tables! *(Calls to them.)* Hello! Hello!

LOIS. They look kinda freaked out.

CASS. *(Calls off.)* Don't be scared! We're just a couple ladies in a barrel! Wish us luck!

LOIS. We need more than luck.

CASS. That's true. We need one of those God-things to save us.

LOIS. The thing is, those God-things aren't actually so reliable.

CASS. Captain Mike's was. He said he went over and all his questions were answered. Life was clear after that. I'm gonna get me one of those ones!

LOIS. Okay, enough! I *get* it! You're devastated, you're unmoored, you're searching for whatever! Now get over it!

CASS. You're yelling at me. These could be our final moments together and —

LOIS. Final, my ass! Open this. *(She pulls gift out of barrel.)*

CASS. Oh, you brought it with! No wonder you're uncomfortable.

LOIS. Unwrap it fast. Now I have been very patient with you, and I thought maybe the shock of the river would snap you out of this thing you're in but —

CASS. *(Having unwrapped gift.)* It's a parachute.

LOIS. And it's a damn good thing I brought it.

CASS. Where'd you get a parachute?

LOIS. Ya-Ya knows people.

CASS. So sweet.

LOIS. Now listen to me, I'm gonna strap this thing on, and you're gonna hold onto me as tight as you can.

CASS. I can't believe I didn't notice that big gift in the barrel.

LOIS. As soon as we go over, I'm gonna pull the ripcord, and we're gonna sail right over everything.

CASS. I thought you were gonna kill yourself?

LOIS. I'm over that.

CASS. What about Ted?

LOIS. Screw Ted! He's on a camel somewhere! You think he's worried about me? You gonna parachute or not?

CASS. But if I don't go over, I won't know if I was meant to go on.

LOIS. *Hello!* Your friend brought a parachute! What are the odds of that? You were meant to go on! Okay?!

CASS. *(Pause.)* Okay.

LOIS. Great! Now help me put it on! *(Cass and Lois struggle with the parachute over the next few lines.)*

CASS. I like this new Lois. Where'd she come from?

LOIS. Captain Mike made some very good points before he got shot.

CASS. Yes he did. *(The barrel pitches suddenly to one side. The women scream and fumble the parachute, which falls and disappears into the river with a SPLASH! Pause.)* Oopsy.

LOIS. Goddamnit!

CASS. Okay, don't panic!

LOIS. Why not, you got a spare parachute on ya?!

CASS. I'll look through the book, maybe there are survival hints!

LOIS. This is what I get for trying to help someone out!

CASS. Stay calm! People *do* survive this, ya know! *(Cass flips through the book frantically. The sound continues to get louder and louder until the end of the play. They have to yell over the roar of The Falls.)* What's this?!

LOIS. *(Looks at book.)* It's a picture of someone in a barrel! The book's full of 'em!

CASS. Right! But they're nailing a lid on it! *(Beat.)* Were we supposed to have a lid?!

LOIS. I don't know!

CASS. Wait, listen. *(Reads from book.)* "Without the customary lid nailed on, Niagara enthusiasts will certainly be dumped from their vessels and crushed on the rocks below!" Did you read this book?!

LOIS. I *skimmed* it! *(The current picks up dramatically. The barrel pitches. The women scream.)*

CASS and LOIS. Whooooaaa!

LOIS. *(To the heavens.)* Okay, you win! *(Tosses her flask in the river.)* No more booze!

CASS. Why'd you do that?!

LOIS. I've stopped drinking!

CASS. You can't stop drinking, you're an alcoholic!

Well, I'm turning over a new leaf!

Yeah, it doesn't really work like that!

(Back out front.) I can see the edge!

CASS. At least I'll get my answer!

LOIS. Heeeeeelp!

CASS. They'll either pull us out of the water in pieces or as whole and perfect as newborn babies!

LOIS. Hold on!

CASS. But whatever happens, the result will be unmistakable!

LOIS. Here it comes! Here it comes! Here it — ! *(Suddenly there's a thud. The barrel stops. The women jerk forward. The waterfall is still roaring, but the barrel has stopped moving. They look around confused.)*

CASS. Well, hells bells.

LOIS. What happened?!

CASS. We stopped!

LOIS. How come?!

CASS. We're stuck!

LOIS. Stuck?!

CASS. On a big rock!

LOIS. Oh! *(They both look around. Odd.)*

CASS. Does this seem strange to you?!

LOIS. Compared to *what?!*

CASS. It doesn't seem odd that we didn't go over?!

LOIS. Not really, no!

CASS. It's like this boulder was *waiting* for us!

LOIS. Please don't jostle the barrel!

CASS. Maybe this is my answer! Maybe this is the hand of God Captain Mike was talking about!

LOIS. Or maybe it's just a rock! *(Cass considers this. Everything seems to drain out of her.)*

CASS. Right.

LOIS. Heeeeeeeeeelp! *(Looks over the edge.)* It's a long way down, isn't it?! *(Calls again.)* Someone heeeeeeelp!

CASS. *(Pause.)* When does the clarity come?

LOIS. *(Beat.)* Do you see that? *(Points DSR.)*

CASS. The sun?

LOIS. Yes. It came up. And you're breathing. What else do you want? *(Cass has no response. Lois has made a good point. Something changes.)*

CASS. Some breakfast would be nice. *(Pause, and then points DSL.)* What are those gardens?

LOIS. That's Canada.

CASS. Oh. It really *is* prettier on that side.

LOIS. Yes it is. Maybe we can have breakfast over there.

CASS. I'd like that. *(They look around, taking in the whole panorama as if for the first time. They breathe easily.)* It's a nice view.

LOIS. That's true. *(The women stay in the barrel, taking in the view. The overwhelming roar of The Falls rises as the lights slowly fade.)*

End of Play

PROPERTY LIST

Vase
Suitcase, clothes (CASS)
Aspic on tray (KIP)
Barrel, wrapped in blankets (LOIS)
List (CASS)
Spoon (LOIS)
Flask (LOIS)
Guidebook (LOIS, CASS)
Pen and paper (LOIS)
Pillow (CASS)
Macramé purse (LOIS)
Ice (LOIS)
Blanket, remote control (KIP)
Camera, wig (BARBARA)
Money (CASS)
Camera (GLEN)
Cell phone (KARLA)
Microphone (CAPTAIN)
Tiny empty liquor bottles (LOIS)
Box of groceries with large can of Spaghettios, large bag of
    Cheetos (CAPTAIN)
Blanket (LOIS)
Handheld tape recorder (KARLA)
Iron (LOIS)
Notebook, pen (KARLA)
I.D. (KARLA)
Kleenex (KIP)
Binoculars (KARLA)
Fake beards (KARLA, GLEN)
Barbie head (CASS)
Glass, liquor (LOIS)
Box with photo album, champagne glasses, swim trunks, book
    of Neruda poems, waffle iron, two caricatures (KIP)
Wig (CASS)
Menus (WAITRESS)

Crowns (CASS, CAPTAIN)
Envelope with money (KIP)
Scythe (WAITRESS)
Tray of food with large chicken leg (WAITRESS)
Check (WAITRESS)
Covered platter with shoeshine kit (GLEN)
Gun (GLEN, LOIS)
Permit (GLEN)
Parachute wrapped as gift (LOIS)
Briefcase (JANIE)
Rubber knife (JANIE)
Scotch and soda, glass (KARLA)
List and pen (JANIE)
Abacus (JANIE)
Bike horn (JANIE)
Cue cards, markers, questions (JANIE)
Bells, whistles, buzzers, two tape recorders (JANIE)
Watch (JANIE)
Towels (KIP)

SOUND EFFECTS

_____ yn Monroe movie
Door slam
Ice machine
Voices on wedding video, organ music, sound of tape rewinding
Roar of Niagara Falls
Foghorn
Crowd cheering
Door knock
Key in lock
"Close to You" by The Carpenters on radio
Helicopter motor
Medieval music
Drums
Rattling chains, ghost sounds, haunted house noises
Game-show music
Buzzer
Applause
Bell dings
"Awww" sound
Gun shots
Vase exploding
Sirens
Splash
Thud